THE LIFE CYCLE OF A CLOWN FISH

By L. L. Owens

Published by The Child's World®
1980 Lookout Drive
Mankato, MN 56003-1705
800-599-READ
www.childsworld.com

The Child's World®: Mary Berendes, Publishing Director
The Design Lab: Kathleen Petelinsek, design
Red Line Editorial: Editorial direction

Photographs ©: iStockphoto, cover (top right, bottom left, bottom right), 1 (top right, bottom left, bottom right); Rodger Klein/Photolibrary, cover (top left), 1 (top left), 13, 30 (bottom); Shutterstock Images, 3, 9, 22; Jodi Jacobson/iStockphoto, 5; Luis Fernando Curci Chavier/Shutterstock Images, 6; Fotolia, 10; D. Kucharski & K. Kucharska/Shutterstock Images, 14; Rich Carey/Shutterstock Images, 17; Carol Buchanan/Photolibrary, 18; Stubblefield Photography/Shutterstock Images, 21; 123RF, 25, 31 (top); Bigstock, 26, 30 (top); Anna Segeren/Shutterstock Images, 29, 31 (bottom)

ISBN: 978-1-60973-145-8
LCCN: 2011927714

Printed in the United States of America
Mankato, MN
July 2011
PA02089

CONTENTS

LIFE CYCLES

Every living thing has a life cycle. A life cycle is the steps a living thing goes through as it grows and changes. Humans have a life cycle. Animals have a life cycle. Plants have a life cycle, too.

A cycle is something that happens over and over again. A life cycle begins with the start of a new life. It continues as a plant or creature grows. And it keeps going as one living thing creates another, or **reproduces**—and the cycle starts over again.

A clown fish's life cycle has four main steps: egg, **larva**, juvenile, and adult clown fish.

There are many kinds of clown fish. Each type goes through the same four life cycle steps.

A clown fish's side fins are called **pectoral fins**.

CLOWN FISH

Like all fish, the clown fish has a backbone that supports its soft body. A tail fin pushes the fish through the water. Side and back fins are for steering and balance. Clown fish have gills on the sides of their heads. Water passes over the gills, which take oxygen from the water so the fish can breathe.

Like sharks and other fish, clown fish are cold-blooded. This means clown fish take on the temperature of their environment. So when it's warm in the ocean, clown fish are warm, too. Clown fish live in the warm waters of the Pacific and Indian Oceans. These tropical waters never get cold enough to freeze. Underwater plants can grow year-round.

Clown fish live in shallow salt water near colorful **coral reefs**. And these reefs are home to some of the world's most colorful animals.

Coral reefs are full of life.

One colorful species is called the pink skunk clown fish.

The clown fish was named for its bright, cheerful appearance. The best-known type of clown fish is orange. Its body has three white stripes lined in black. Other striking clown fish species can be red, pink, black, yellow, or blue. Some people think clown fish look like they are wearing costumes.

An adult clown fish can grow to be about 4 inches (10.2 cm) long. Tough scales protect the fish's soft body. There are about 28 different kinds of clown fish.

HATCHING

The life cycle of a clown fish begins with a **fertilized** egg. When the clown fish **hatches** out of its silvery egg, it does not look like an adult. It has a tiny, almost see-through body and large, dark eyes. This hatchling is called a larva.

All clown fish larvae are born male. But they are not able to reproduce yet.

Tiny clown fish eggs are ready to hatch.

This rotifer is a tiny organism seen through a **microscope**. Clown fish larvae feed on plankton, including rotifers.

NEW CLOWN FISH

Newborn larvae do not eat for the first day or so. Yolk sacs from their eggs are still attached to their bodies. The yolk sacs provide all the nourishment the larvae need.

After the yolk sac is gone, clown fish larvae float toward the top of the water and begin to eat plankton. These are tiny organisms that float near the surface of the water. But not all larvae survive. Many are eaten by bigger fish.

After about a week or two, the clown fish larvae quickly begin to change as they go through **metamorphosis**. Their bodies start to become colorful. They look like little clown fish. At around this time, the clown fish begin swimming by flipping their fins back and forth. These fish are called juveniles.

At the ocean floor, the juveniles form groups. Some of the fish will stop changing, but others will become adults. A clown fish can enter the adult stage anywhere from a few months to several years old.

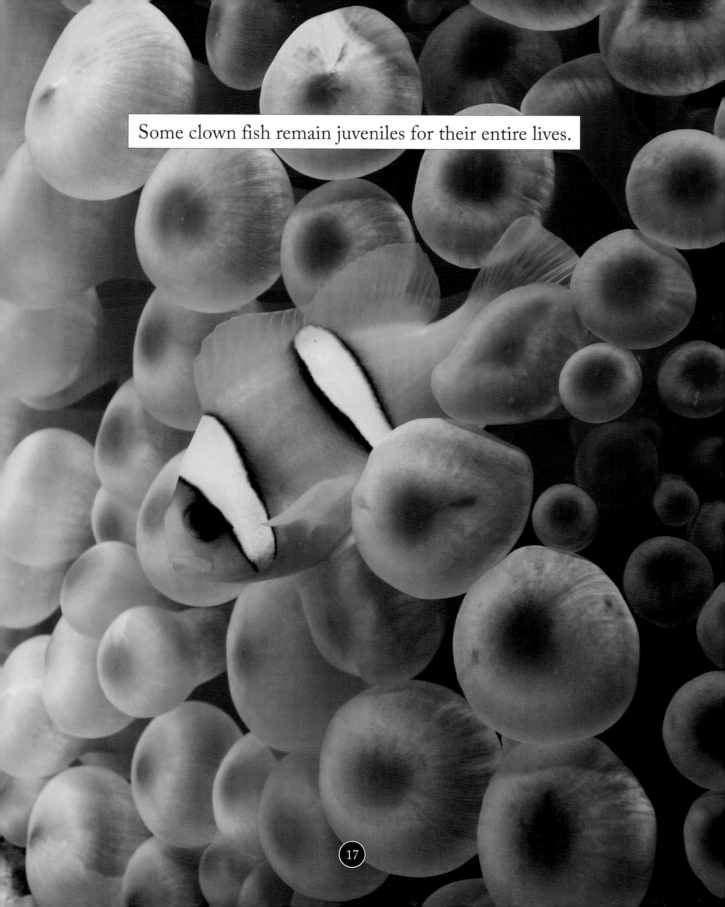

Some clown fish remain juveniles for their entire lives.

A female (top) and a male are the heads of a clown fish group.

A clown fish group includes one adult female, one adult male, and some juvenile males. Where does the female come from? The largest male clown fish in a group transforms into a female. That female then pairs up with the next-largest male. This male develops into an adult to reproduce. Once a fish is female, it cannot change back to a male.

The rest of the fish in the group are juvenile males that cannot reproduce. When the female dies, her male mate changes into a female. Then, the next biggest male matures and becomes her mate.

A SAFE HOME

To stay safe from ocean **predators**, clown fish need a secure home. They live in small groups among creatures called sea **anemones**. Clown fish spend so much time around anemones that they are also known as anemonefish.

Coral reefs are home to many anemones. Anemones look like flowering plants, but they are actually animals. They have many arm-like **tentacles** that sway in the water currents.

Each small group of clown fish lives in the shelter of just one anemone. And some anemones will only shelter certain kinds of clown fish.

The spinecheek clown fish lives with the bulb tentacle anemone.

An anemone uses its tentacles to sting and capture food,
but the clown fish that live with the anemone are safe.

Sea anemones make a unique home. Clown fish are safe living with anemones, but other fish are not. Anemones use their tentacles to sting fish that would otherwise eat clown fish.

Anemones sting clown fish, too. But clown fish are covered in a layer of special slime. The slime protects them from being hurt by the anemone's poisonous sting.

Sea anemones and clown fish have a **symbiotic** relationship. That means they both benefit from living together.

An anemone protects clown fish, but clown fish help an anemone, too. The colorful clown fish attract larger fish. When a fish swims nearby, the anemone stings it with its tentacles. Then the anemone eats its meal.

After the anemone eats, clown fish help it stay clean. Leftover bits of plant or fish meals may get stuck on the anemone's tentacles. Clown fish eat these leftover bits, which keeps the anemone clean and healthy. This feeds the clown fish, too!

A clown fish's bright colors attract other fish to come near an anemone. This helps the anemone get food.

Clown fish lay their eggs on a rock near an anemone.

CLOWN FISH PAIRS

Male-female clown fish pairs may stay together for life. Before another generation's life cycle can begin, these pairs need to reproduce, or create baby clown fish.

The male and female prepare a nest. They clean an area of rock very close to an anemone. Then, the female lays up to 1,000 eggs. The male swims over the nest. He releases sperm to **fertilize** the eggs. Then the eggs can begin to grow into a new generation of fish. The male keeps watch over the nest, keeps it clean, and eats any eggs that die off. Inside the eggs that survive, tiny creatures are beginning to grow.

Clown fish eggs hatch in about one week. The parent fish do not take care of the hatched larvae.

In nature, clown fish can live to age ten. Those living in aquariums can survive for up to 18 years.

Many eggs will be laid and new clown fish will hatch. The life cycle of the clown fish continues.

A clown fish juvenile might become an adult that reproduces.

LIFE CYCLE DIAGRAM

Egg

Larva

Adult Clown Fish

Juvenile

Web Sites

Visit our Web site for links about the life cycle of a clown fish: **childsworld.com/links**

Note to Parents, Teachers, and Librarians: We routinely verify our Web links to make sure they are safe and active sites. So encourage your readers to check them out!

Books

Head, Honor. *Amazing Fish*. Pleasantville, NY: Gareth Stevens Publishing, 2008.

Ross, Michael Elsohn. *Life Cycles*. Brookfield, CT: Millbrook Press, 2001.

Sexton, Colleen. *Clown Fish*. Minneapolis, MN: Bellwether Media, 2007.

Glossary

anemones (uh-NEM-uh-neez): Anemones are saltwater sea animals that catch food by stinging it with tentacles. Clown fish live in small groups among sea anemones.

coral reefs (KOR-uhl REEFZ): Coral reefs are underwater communities built of skeletons of tiny coral animals, where many fish and other animals live. Clown fish live near coral reefs.

fertilized (FUR-tuh-lyzd): Fertilized refers to an egg that can grow and develop into a new life. A clown fish's life cycle begins with a fertilized egg.

hatches (HACH-ez): When something hatches, it breaks out of an egg. When a clown fish hatches, it does not look like an adult.

larva (LAR-vuh): A larva is an animal soon after hatching that looks very different from its parents. A clown fish larva eats plankton.

metamorphosis (met-uh-MOR-fuh-siss): Metamorphosis is the series of changes some animals go through between hatching and adulthood. A clown fish becomes colorful as it goes through metamorphosis.

microscope (MYE-kruh-skope): A microscope is a tool for making small things look bigger. Some types of plankton are so small, they can only be seen through a microscope.

pectoral fins (pek-TO-ruhl FINZ): Pectoral fins are a fish's side fins. A clown fish's pectoral fins and back fins are for steering and balance.

predators (PRED-uh-turs): Predators are animals that hunt and eat other animals. Clown fish live near anemones to stay safe from predators.

symbiotic (sim-bee-AH-tic): A symbiotic relationship is when two kinds of animals live closely together in a way that helps both. Clown fish and anemones have a symbiotic relationship.

tentacles (TEN-tuh-kullz): Tentacles are long feelers or limbs that come out from the bodies of some animals. Anemones use their tentacles to sting fish.

32